50 Easy Cakes for Any Celebration

By: Kelly Johnson

Table of Contents

- Classic Vanilla Birthday Cake
- Chocolate Fudge Cake
- Lemon Poppy Seed Cake
- Red Velvet Cake
- Carrot Cake with Cream Cheese Frosting
- Funfetti Cake
- Strawberry Shortcake
- Coconut Cream Cake
- Marble Cake
- Chocolate Peanut Butter Cake
- Coffee and Walnut Cake
- Almond Cake with Raspberry Jam
- Pineapple Upside-Down Cake
- Tiramisu Cake
- Angel Food Cake
- Vanilla Bean Pound Cake
- Zebra Cake
- Key Lime Cake
- Mocha Cake
- German Chocolate Cake
- Chocolate Lava Cake
- Blueberry Lemon Cake
- Cheesecake with Mixed Berries
- Banana Cake with Brown Sugar Frosting
- Spice Cake with Cream Cheese Frosting
- Pina Colada Cake
- Funfetti Bundt Cake
- Chocolate Coconut Cake
- Apple Cinnamon Cake
- Raspberry Almond Cake
- Black Forest Cake
- Hazelnut Cake with Chocolate Ganache
- Snickerdoodle Cake
- Lemon Blueberry Cake
- Vanilla Cupcakes with Buttercream Frosting

- Pistachio Cake
- Coconut Lime Cake
- Maple Pecan Cake
- Peach Cobbler Cake
- Nutella Swirl Cake
- Churro Cake
- White Chocolate Raspberry Cake
- Double Chocolate Chip Cake
- Pumpkin Spice Cake
- Mocha Hazelnut Cake
- Cream Puff Cake
- Chocolate Mint Cake
- Cinnamon Roll Cake
- Chocolate Cherry Cake
- Chocolate Raspberry Bundt Cake

Classic Vanilla Birthday Cake

Ingredients:

- 2 1/2 cups all-purpose flour
- 2 1/2 tsp baking powder
- 1/2 tsp salt
- 1 cup unsalted butter, softened
- 2 cups granulated sugar
- 4 large eggs
- 1 tbsp vanilla extract
- 1 cup whole milk

Instructions:

1. Preheat your oven to 350°F (175°C). Grease and flour two 9-inch round cake pans.
2. In a bowl, whisk together the flour, baking powder, and salt.
3. In a separate bowl, beat the butter and sugar together until light and fluffy, about 3-4 minutes.
4. Add the eggs one at a time, beating well after each addition. Stir in the vanilla extract.
5. Gradually add the dry ingredients, alternating with the milk, starting and ending with the dry ingredients. Mix until just combined.
6. Divide the batter evenly between the prepared pans.
7. Bake for 25-30 minutes, or until a toothpick inserted into the center comes out clean.
8. Let the cakes cool in the pans for 10 minutes, then transfer to a wire rack to cool completely. Frost with your favorite buttercream.

Chocolate Fudge Cake

Ingredients:

- 2 cups all-purpose flour
- 1 1/2 cups granulated sugar
- 3/4 cup unsweetened cocoa powder
- 1 1/2 tsp baking powder
- 1 1/2 tsp baking soda
- 1 tsp salt
- 2 large eggs
- 1 cup buttermilk
- 1/2 cup vegetable oil
- 2 tsp vanilla extract
- 1 cup boiling water

Instructions:

1. Preheat your oven to 350°F (175°C). Grease and flour two 9-inch round cake pans.
2. In a large bowl, mix together the flour, sugar, cocoa powder, baking powder, baking soda, and salt.
3. Add the eggs, buttermilk, vegetable oil, and vanilla extract, and beat until smooth.
4. Stir in the boiling water. The batter will be thin, but that's okay.
5. Pour the batter into the prepared pans.
6. Bake for 30-35 minutes, or until a toothpick inserted into the center comes out clean.
7. Allow the cakes to cool in the pans for 10 minutes, then transfer to a wire rack to cool completely. Frost with your favorite chocolate frosting.

Lemon Poppy Seed Cake

Ingredients:

- 2 1/2 cups all-purpose flour
- 2 tsp baking powder
- 1/2 tsp baking soda
- 1/2 tsp salt
- 1/4 cup poppy seeds
- 1 cup unsalted butter, softened
- 2 cups granulated sugar
- 4 large eggs
- 1/2 cup fresh lemon juice
- Zest of 2 lemons
- 1 cup buttermilk

Instructions:

1. Preheat your oven to 350°F (175°C). Grease and flour a 9x13-inch baking dish or two 9-inch round cake pans.
2. In a bowl, whisk together the flour, baking powder, baking soda, salt, and poppy seeds.
3. In a separate bowl, cream the butter and sugar until light and fluffy.
4. Add the eggs, one at a time, beating well after each addition.
5. Stir in the lemon juice and zest.
6. Alternately add the dry ingredients and buttermilk, starting and ending with the dry ingredients.
7. Pour the batter into the prepared pan(s).
8. Bake for 30-35 minutes, or until a toothpick inserted into the center comes out clean.
9. Let the cake cool completely before frosting with a lemon glaze or cream cheese frosting.

Red Velvet Cake

Ingredients:

- 2 1/2 cups all-purpose flour
- 1 1/2 cups granulated sugar
- 1 tsp baking soda
- 1 tsp cocoa powder
- 1 tsp salt
- 1 1/2 cups vegetable oil
- 1 cup buttermilk
- 2 large eggs
- 2 tbsp red food coloring
- 1 tsp vanilla extract
- 1 tsp white vinegar

Instructions:

1. Preheat your oven to 350°F (175°C). Grease and flour two 9-inch round cake pans.
2. In a bowl, mix the flour, sugar, baking soda, cocoa powder, and salt.
3. In a separate bowl, combine the oil, buttermilk, eggs, food coloring, vanilla, and vinegar.
4. Gradually add the wet ingredients to the dry ingredients, mixing until smooth.
5. Divide the batter evenly between the prepared pans.
6. Bake for 25-30 minutes, or until a toothpick inserted into the center comes out clean.
7. Let the cakes cool in the pans for 10 minutes, then transfer to a wire rack to cool completely. Frost with cream cheese frosting.

Carrot Cake with Cream Cheese Frosting

Ingredients:

- 2 cups all-purpose flour
- 2 tsp baking powder
- 1 1/2 tsp baking soda
- 1 tsp cinnamon
- 1/2 tsp salt
- 4 large eggs
- 1 1/2 cups vegetable oil
- 2 cups granulated sugar
- 3 cups grated carrots
- 1 cup walnuts or pecans (optional)
- 1 tsp vanilla extract

For the Cream Cheese Frosting:

- 8 oz cream cheese, softened
- 1/2 cup unsalted butter, softened
- 4 cups powdered sugar
- 1 tsp vanilla extract

Instructions:

1. Preheat your oven to 350°F (175°C). Grease and flour two 9-inch round cake pans.
2. In a bowl, whisk together the flour, baking powder, baking soda, cinnamon, and salt.
3. In a separate bowl, beat the eggs, oil, and sugar until combined.
4. Stir in the grated carrots, nuts (if using), and vanilla extract.
5. Gradually add the dry ingredients and mix until just combined.
6. Pour the batter into the prepared pans.
7. Bake for 25-30 minutes, or until a toothpick inserted into the center comes out clean.
8. For the frosting, beat the cream cheese and butter until smooth. Gradually add powdered sugar and vanilla, and beat until fluffy.
9. Frost the cooled cakes with cream cheese frosting.

Funfetti Cake

Ingredients:

- 2 1/2 cups all-purpose flour
- 1 1/2 cups granulated sugar
- 1 tbsp baking powder
- 1/2 tsp salt
- 1 cup unsalted butter, softened
- 4 large eggs
- 1 cup whole milk
- 1 tbsp vanilla extract
- 1/2 cup rainbow sprinkles

Instructions:

1. Preheat your oven to 350°F (175°C). Grease and flour two 9-inch round cake pans.
2. In a bowl, whisk together the flour, sugar, baking powder, and salt.
3. In a separate bowl, beat the butter and sugar together until light and fluffy.
4. Add the eggs one at a time, beating well after each addition.
5. Stir in the milk and vanilla extract.
6. Gradually add the dry ingredients to the wet ingredients and mix until smooth.
7. Gently fold in the rainbow sprinkles.
8. Divide the batter between the prepared pans.
9. Bake for 25-30 minutes, or until a toothpick inserted into the center comes out clean.
10. Allow the cakes to cool completely before frosting with vanilla buttercream and additional sprinkles.

Strawberry Shortcake

Ingredients:

- 2 cups all-purpose flour
- 1 tbsp baking powder
- 1/4 cup granulated sugar
- 1/2 tsp salt
- 1/2 cup unsalted butter, cold and cut into cubes
- 2/3 cup heavy cream
- 1 tsp vanilla extract
- 2 cups fresh strawberries, sliced
- 1/4 cup powdered sugar
- Whipped cream for topping

Instructions:

1. Preheat your oven to 375°F (190°C). Grease and flour an 8-inch round cake pan.
2. In a bowl, whisk together the flour, baking powder, sugar, and salt.
3. Cut in the cold butter using a pastry cutter or fork until the mixture resembles coarse crumbs.
4. Stir in the heavy cream and vanilla until just combined.
5. Turn the dough out onto a floured surface and gently knead until it comes together. Pat it into a 1-inch thick circle and cut out rounds using a biscuit cutter.
6. Place the rounds on a baking sheet and bake for 15-18 minutes, until golden brown.
7. Whip the cream with powdered sugar until stiff peaks form.
8. Assemble the shortcakes by slicing them in half, topping with strawberries, and a dollop of whipped cream.

Coconut Cream Cake

Ingredients:

- 2 1/2 cups all-purpose flour
- 2 tsp baking powder
- 1/2 tsp salt
- 1 cup unsalted butter, softened
- 2 cups granulated sugar
- 4 large eggs
- 1 cup coconut milk
- 1 tsp vanilla extract
- 1 1/2 cups shredded coconut

Instructions:

1. Preheat your oven to 350°F (175°C). Grease and flour two 9-inch round cake pans.
2. In a bowl, whisk together the flour, baking powder, and salt.
3. In a separate bowl, cream the butter and sugar until light and fluffy.
4. Add the eggs one at a time, beating well after each addition.
5. Stir in the coconut milk and vanilla extract.
6. Gradually add the dry ingredients and mix until just combined.
7. Fold in the shredded coconut.
8. Pour the batter into the prepared pans.
9. Bake for 25-30 minutes, or until a toothpick inserted into the center comes out clean.
10. Frost with whipped cream or cream cheese frosting and top with additional coconut.

Marble Cake

Ingredients:

- 2 1/2 cups all-purpose flour
- 2 tsp baking powder
- 1/2 tsp salt
- 1 cup unsalted butter, softened
- 2 cups granulated sugar
- 4 large eggs
- 1 cup whole milk
- 2 tsp vanilla extract
- 1/4 cup unsweetened cocoa powder

Instructions:

1. Preheat your oven to 350°F (175°C). Grease and flour two 9-inch round cake pans.
2. In a bowl, whisk together the flour, baking powder, and salt.
3. In a separate bowl, beat the butter and sugar until light and fluffy.
4. Add the eggs, one at a time, beating well after each addition.
5. Stir in the milk and vanilla extract.
6. Divide the batter into two bowls. Add cocoa powder to one half and mix well.
7. Alternately spoon the vanilla and chocolate batters into the pans, swirling with a knife to create a marble effect.
8. Bake for 25-30 minutes, or until a toothpick inserted into the center comes out clean.
9. Allow the cakes to cool before frosting.

Chocolate Peanut Butter Cake

Ingredients:

- **For the cake:**
    - 2 cups all-purpose flour
    - 2 cups granulated sugar
    - 1 cup unsweetened cocoa powder
    - 1 1/2 tsp baking powder
    - 1 1/2 tsp baking soda
    - 1/2 tsp salt
    - 2 large eggs
    - 1 cup buttermilk
    - 1/2 cup vegetable oil
    - 1 tsp vanilla extract
    - 1 cup boiling water
- **For the peanut butter frosting:**
    - 1 cup unsalted butter, softened
    - 1 cup creamy peanut butter
    - 4 cups powdered sugar
    - 2-4 tbsp milk
    - 1 tsp vanilla extract

Instructions:

1. Preheat your oven to 350°F (175°C). Grease and flour two 9-inch round cake pans.
2. In a large bowl, whisk together the flour, sugar, cocoa powder, baking powder, baking soda, and salt.
3. Add the eggs, buttermilk, oil, and vanilla extract, and beat until smooth.
4. Gradually add the boiling water, mixing until combined. The batter will be thin.
5. Pour the batter into the prepared pans and bake for 30-35 minutes, or until a toothpick inserted into the center comes out clean.
6. Let the cakes cool in the pans for 10 minutes, then transfer to a wire rack to cool completely.
7. For the frosting, beat the butter and peanut butter together until smooth. Gradually add the powdered sugar, alternating with milk, and beat until creamy.
8. Frost the cooled cakes with the peanut butter frosting.

Coffee and Walnut Cake

Ingredients:

- 2 cups all-purpose flour
- 1 tsp baking powder
- 1/2 tsp baking soda
- 1/2 tsp salt
- 1 tbsp instant coffee granules
- 2 tbsp hot water
- 1/2 cup unsalted butter, softened
- 1 cup granulated sugar
- 2 large eggs
- 1/2 cup milk
- 1 tsp vanilla extract
- 1 cup chopped walnuts
- **For the frosting:**
    - 1 cup unsalted butter, softened
    - 2 cups powdered sugar
    - 2 tbsp strong brewed coffee
    - 1/2 tsp vanilla extract

Instructions:

1. Preheat your oven to 350°F (175°C). Grease and flour two 9-inch round cake pans.
2. Dissolve the coffee granules in hot water and set aside.
3. In a bowl, whisk together the flour, baking powder, baking soda, and salt.
4. In a separate bowl, cream the butter and sugar together until light and fluffy.
5. Beat in the eggs, one at a time, then stir in the coffee and vanilla extract.
6. Gradually add the dry ingredients, alternating with the milk, until just combined.
7. Fold in the chopped walnuts.
8. Divide the batter between the prepared pans and bake for 25-30 minutes, or until a toothpick inserted into the center comes out clean.
9. For the frosting, beat the butter and powdered sugar together. Gradually add the brewed coffee and vanilla extract, and beat until smooth.
10. Frost the cooled cakes and garnish with additional chopped walnuts.

Almond Cake with Raspberry Jam

Ingredients:

- 2 cups all-purpose flour
- 1 tsp baking powder
- 1/2 tsp salt
- 1 cup unsalted butter, softened
- 1 1/2 cups granulated sugar
- 4 large eggs
- 1 tsp vanilla extract
- 1 tsp almond extract
- 1/2 cup whole milk
- 1/2 cup raspberry jam
- **For the frosting:**
    - 1 cup heavy cream
    - 2 tbsp powdered sugar
    - 1/2 tsp vanilla extract

Instructions:

1. Preheat your oven to 350°F (175°C). Grease and flour two 9-inch round cake pans.
2. In a bowl, whisk together the flour, baking powder, and salt.
3. In a separate bowl, beat the butter and sugar together until light and fluffy.
4. Add the eggs one at a time, beating well after each addition. Stir in the vanilla and almond extract.
5. Gradually add the dry ingredients, alternating with the milk, until just combined.
6. Divide the batter between the prepared pans and bake for 25-30 minutes, or until a toothpick inserted into the center comes out clean.
7. Let the cakes cool in the pans for 10 minutes, then transfer to a wire rack to cool completely.
8. For the frosting, beat the heavy cream with powdered sugar and vanilla extract until stiff peaks form.
9. Once the cakes are cool, spread a layer of raspberry jam on top of one cake layer, then top with the second cake layer.
10. Frost the cake with whipped cream and garnish with raspberries or almonds.

Pineapple Upside-Down Cake

Ingredients:

- 1/2 cup unsalted butter, melted
- 1 cup packed brown sugar
- 1 can (20 oz) pineapple rings, drained
- Maraschino cherries (optional)
- 1 1/2 cups all-purpose flour
- 2 tsp baking powder
- 1/2 tsp salt
- 1/2 cup granulated sugar
- 2 large eggs
- 1 tsp vanilla extract
- 1/2 cup whole milk

Instructions:

1. Preheat your oven to 350°F (175°C). Grease and lightly flour a 9-inch round cake pan.
2. Pour the melted butter into the bottom of the cake pan, and sprinkle the brown sugar evenly over the butter.
3. Arrange the pineapple rings over the brown sugar mixture, and place a cherry in the center of each pineapple ring.
4. In a bowl, whisk together the flour, baking powder, and salt.
5. In a separate bowl, beat the granulated sugar and eggs until light and fluffy. Stir in the vanilla extract.
6. Add the dry ingredients, alternating with the milk, and mix until just combined.
7. Pour the batter over the pineapple rings in the pan.
8. Bake for 30-35 minutes, or until a toothpick inserted into the center comes out clean.
9. Let the cake cool in the pan for 5 minutes, then carefully invert onto a serving plate.

Tiramisu Cake

Ingredients:

- **For the cake:**
    - 2 cups all-purpose flour
    - 1 tsp baking powder
    - 1/2 tsp baking soda
    - 1/2 tsp salt
    - 1 cup unsalted butter, softened
    - 1 1/2 cups granulated sugar
    - 3 large eggs
    - 1 cup strong brewed coffee, cooled
    - 2 tbsp coffee liqueur (optional)
    - 1 tsp vanilla extract
- **For the mascarpone filling:**
    - 1 cup mascarpone cheese
    - 1 cup heavy cream
    - 1/2 cup powdered sugar
    - 1 tsp vanilla extract

Instructions:

1. Preheat your oven to 350°F (175°C). Grease and flour two 9-inch round cake pans.
2. In a bowl, whisk together the flour, baking powder, baking soda, and salt.
3. In a separate bowl, cream the butter and sugar until light and fluffy.
4. Add the eggs one at a time, beating well after each addition.
5. Gradually add the dry ingredients, alternating with the coffee, coffee liqueur, and vanilla extract, until just combined.
6. Divide the batter between the prepared pans and bake for 25-30 minutes, or until a toothpick inserted into the center comes out clean.
7. Let the cakes cool in the pans for 10 minutes, then transfer to a wire rack to cool completely.
8. For the filling, whip the mascarpone, heavy cream, powdered sugar, and vanilla extract until stiff peaks form.
9. Once the cakes are cooled, slice each cake in half horizontally.
10. Layer the cake with mascarpone filling and drizzle with additional coffee or coffee liqueur.

Angel Food Cake

Ingredients:

- 1 cup cake flour
- 1 1/2 cups granulated sugar
- 1/2 tsp salt
- 1 1/2 tsp cream of tartar
- 1 tsp vanilla extract
- 12 large egg whites (at room temperature)
- 1/2 tsp almond extract

Instructions:

1. Preheat your oven to 350°F (175°C). Do not grease an angel food cake pan.
2. In a bowl, whisk together the flour, 3/4 cup sugar, and salt.
3. In a separate bowl, beat the egg whites with cream of tartar until soft peaks form. Gradually add the remaining sugar, continuing to beat until stiff peaks form.
4. Fold in the vanilla and almond extract.
5. Gradually fold in the flour mixture in batches until combined.
6. Pour the batter into the ungreased pan and spread it evenly.
7. Bake for 35-40 minutes, or until the cake springs back when lightly touched.
8. Let the cake cool upside down on a wire rack for about an hour, then carefully remove from the pan.

Vanilla Bean Pound Cake

Ingredients:

- 2 1/2 cups all-purpose flour
- 1 1/2 tsp baking powder
- 1/2 tsp salt
- 1 cup unsalted butter, softened
- 2 cups granulated sugar
- 4 large eggs
- 1 tbsp vanilla bean paste
- 1/2 cup whole milk

Instructions:

1. Preheat your oven to 350°F (175°C). Grease and flour a 9x5-inch loaf pan.
2. In a bowl, whisk together the flour, baking powder, and salt.
3. In a separate bowl, cream the butter and sugar until light and fluffy.
4. Add the eggs one at a time, beating well after each addition.
5. Stir in the vanilla bean paste.
6. Gradually add the dry ingredients, alternating with the milk, until just combined.
7. Pour the batter into the prepared pan and smooth the top.
8. Bake for 60-70 minutes, or until a toothpick inserted into the center comes out clean.
9. Let the cake cool in the pan for 10 minutes, then transfer to a wire rack to cool completely.

Zebra Cake

Ingredients:

- 2 1/2 cups all-purpose flour
- 2 tsp baking powder
- 1/2 tsp salt
- 1 cup unsalted butter, softened
- 1 1/2 cups granulated sugar
- 4 large eggs
- 1 tsp vanilla extract
- 1 cup whole milk
- 1/4 cup unsweetened cocoa powder

Instructions:

1. Preheat your oven to 350°F (175°C). Grease and flour a 9-inch round cake pan.
2. In a bowl, whisk together the flour, baking powder, and salt.
3. In a separate bowl, cream the butter and sugar until light and fluffy.
4. Add the eggs one at a time, beating well after each addition.
5. Stir in the vanilla extract.
6. Gradually add the dry ingredients, alternating with the milk, until just combined.
7. Divide the batter into two bowls. Stir cocoa powder into one half of the batter.
8. Alternate spooning the vanilla and chocolate batter into the center of the pan to create a zebra pattern.
9. Bake for 25-30 minutes, or until a toothpick inserted into the center comes out clean.

Key Lime Cake

Ingredients:

- 2 1/2 cups all-purpose flour
- 2 tsp baking powder
- 1/2 tsp salt
- 1 cup unsalted butter, softened
- 1 1/2 cups granulated sugar
- 3 large eggs
- 1/4 cup key lime juice
- 1 tbsp lime zest
- 1/2 cup buttermilk

Instructions:

1. Preheat your oven to 350°F (175°C). Grease and flour two 9-inch round cake pans.
2. In a bowl, whisk together the flour, baking powder, and salt.
3. In a separate bowl, cream the butter and sugar together until light and fluffy.
4. Beat in the eggs, one at a time. Stir in the key lime juice and lime zest.
5. Gradually add the dry ingredients, alternating with the buttermilk, until just combined.
6. Divide the batter between the prepared pans and bake for 25-30 minutes, or until a toothpick inserted into the center comes out clean.
7. Let the cakes cool in the pans for 10 minutes, then transfer to a wire rack to cool completely.

Mocha Cake

Ingredients:

- 2 cups all-purpose flour
- 1 1/2 tsp baking soda
- 1/2 tsp baking powder
- 1/2 tsp salt
- 1/2 cup unsweetened cocoa powder
- 1 cup strong brewed coffee, cooled
- 1 cup granulated sugar
- 1/2 cup brown sugar
- 2 large eggs
- 1/2 cup vegetable oil
- 1 tsp vanilla extract

Instructions:

1. Preheat your oven to 350°F (175°C). Grease and flour two 9-inch round cake pans.
2. In a bowl, whisk together the flour, baking soda, baking powder, salt, and cocoa powder.
3. In a separate bowl, whisk together the coffee, sugar, brown sugar, eggs, oil, and vanilla extract.
4. Gradually mix the dry ingredients into the wet ingredients until just combined.
5. Divide the batter between the prepared pans and bake for 25-30 minutes, or until a toothpick inserted into the center comes out clean.
6. Let the cakes cool in the pans for 10 minutes, then transfer to a wire rack to cool completely.

German Chocolate Cake

Ingredients:

- 2 1/2 cups all-purpose flour
- 1 1/2 tsp baking powder
- 1/2 tsp baking soda
- 1/2 tsp salt
- 1 cup unsalted butter, softened
- 2 cups granulated sugar
- 4 large eggs
- 1 tsp vanilla extract
- 1 cup buttermilk
- 1 cup unsweetened cocoa powder
- 1 cup shredded coconut
- 1 cup chopped pecans

Instructions:

1. Preheat your oven to 350°F (175°C). Grease and flour two 9-inch round cake pans.
2. In a bowl, whisk together the flour, baking powder, baking soda, and salt.
3. In a separate bowl, cream together the butter and sugar until light and fluffy.
4. Add the eggs, one at a time, beating well after each addition. Stir in the vanilla extract.
5. Gradually add the dry ingredients, alternating with the buttermilk, until just combined.
6. Stir in the cocoa powder, coconut, and pecans.
7. Divide the batter between the pans and bake for 25-30 minutes, or until a toothpick inserted into the center comes out clean.
8. Let the cakes cool in the pans for 10 minutes, then transfer to a wire rack to cool completely.

Chocolate Lava Cake

Ingredients:

- 1 cup semisweet chocolate chips
- 1/2 cup unsalted butter
- 1/2 cup granulated sugar
- 1/4 cup all-purpose flour
- 2 large eggs
- 2 large egg yolks
- 1 tsp vanilla extract
- Pinch of salt

Instructions:

1. Preheat your oven to 425°F (220°C). Grease four 6-ounce ramekins with butter and dust with flour.
2. In a microwave-safe bowl, melt the chocolate and butter together in 30-second intervals, stirring in between, until smooth.
3. In a separate bowl, whisk the eggs, egg yolks, sugar, flour, vanilla extract, and salt until smooth.
4. Stir the melted chocolate mixture into the egg mixture until well combined.
5. Pour the batter into the prepared ramekins, filling each about 3/4 full.
6. Bake for 12-14 minutes, or until the edges are set but the center is soft.
7. Let cool for 1-2 minutes, then carefully invert the ramekins onto plates to serve.

Blueberry Lemon Cake

Ingredients:

- 2 1/2 cups all-purpose flour
- 1 1/2 tsp baking powder
- 1/2 tsp salt
- 1 cup unsalted butter, softened
- 2 cups granulated sugar
- 4 large eggs
- 2 tbsp lemon zest
- 1/4 cup fresh lemon juice
- 1 cup buttermilk
- 1 1/2 cups fresh blueberries

Instructions:

1. Preheat your oven to 350°F (175°C). Grease and flour two 9-inch round cake pans.
2. In a bowl, whisk together the flour, baking powder, and salt.
3. In a separate bowl, cream the butter and sugar together until light and fluffy.
4. Add the eggs, one at a time, beating well after each addition. Stir in the lemon zest and lemon juice.
5. Gradually add the dry ingredients, alternating with the buttermilk, until just combined.
6. Gently fold in the blueberries.
7. Divide the batter between the prepared pans and bake for 25-30 minutes, or until a toothpick inserted into the center comes out clean.
8. Let the cakes cool in the pans for 10 minutes, then transfer to a wire rack to cool completely.

Cheesecake with Mixed Berries

Ingredients:

- 1 1/2 cups graham cracker crumbs
- 1/4 cup granulated sugar
- 1/2 cup unsalted butter, melted
- 3 (8 oz) packages cream cheese, softened
- 1 cup granulated sugar
- 3 large eggs
- 1 tsp vanilla extract
- 1/4 cup sour cream
- 2 cups mixed berries (strawberries, raspberries, blueberries)

Instructions:

1. Preheat your oven to 325°F (160°C). Grease a 9-inch springform pan.
2. In a bowl, combine the graham cracker crumbs, sugar, and melted butter. Press the mixture into the bottom of the prepared pan.
3. In a separate bowl, beat the cream cheese and sugar until smooth.
4. Add the eggs, one at a time, beating well after each addition. Stir in the vanilla extract and sour cream.
5. Pour the cream cheese mixture into the crust and smooth the top.
6. Bake for 50-60 minutes, or until the center is just set.
7. Let the cheesecake cool to room temperature, then refrigerate for at least 4 hours or overnight.
8. Top with mixed berries before serving.

Banana Cake with Brown Sugar Frosting

Ingredients:

For the Cake

- 2 cups all-purpose flour
- 1 tsp baking powder
- 1/2 tsp baking soda
- 1/2 tsp salt
- 1/2 cup unsalted butter, softened
- 1 1/2 cups granulated sugar
- 3 ripe bananas, mashed
- 2 large eggs
- 1 tsp vanilla extract
- 1/2 cup buttermilk

For the Frosting

- 1/2 cup unsalted butter, softened
- 1/2 cup brown sugar
- 1/4 cup heavy cream
- 1 tsp vanilla extract

Instructions:

1. Preheat your oven to 350°F (175°C). Grease and flour two 9-inch round cake pans.
2. In a bowl, whisk together the flour, baking powder, baking soda, and salt.
3. In a separate bowl, cream the butter and sugar together until light and fluffy.
4. Add the eggs, one at a time, beating well after each addition. Stir in the mashed bananas and vanilla extract.
5. Gradually add the dry ingredients, alternating with the buttermilk, until just combined.
6. Divide the batter between the pans and bake for 25-30 minutes, or until a toothpick inserted into the center comes out clean.
7. Let the cakes cool in the pans for 10 minutes, then transfer to a wire rack to cool completely.
8. For the frosting, melt the butter and brown sugar in a saucepan over medium heat. Stir in the heavy cream and vanilla extract, and bring to a simmer. Cook for 3-4 minutes, stirring constantly.

9. Let the frosting cool slightly before spreading it over the cooled cake.

Spice Cake with Cream Cheese Frosting

Ingredients:

- 2 1/2 cups all-purpose flour
- 1 1/2 tsp baking powder
- 1 1/2 tsp ground cinnamon
- 1 tsp ground ginger
- 1/2 tsp ground cloves
- 1/4 tsp salt
- 1/2 cup unsalted butter, softened
- 1 1/2 cups granulated sugar
- 3 large eggs
- 1 cup buttermilk

For the Cream Cheese Frosting

- 8 oz cream cheese, softened
- 1/2 cup unsalted butter, softened
- 4 cups powdered sugar
- 1 tsp vanilla extract

Instructions:

1. Preheat your oven to 350°F (175°C). Grease and flour two 9-inch round cake pans.
2. In a bowl, whisk together the flour, baking powder, cinnamon, ginger, cloves, and salt.
3. In a separate bowl, cream the butter and sugar together until light and fluffy.
4. Add the eggs, one at a time, beating well after each addition.
5. Gradually add the dry ingredients, alternating with the buttermilk, until just combined.
6. Divide the batter between the pans and bake for 25-30 minutes, or until a toothpick inserted into the center comes out clean.
7. Let the cakes cool in the pans for 10 minutes, then transfer to a wire rack to cool completely.
8. For the frosting, beat the cream cheese and butter together until smooth. Gradually add the powdered sugar and vanilla extract, and beat until fluffy.
9. Frost the cooled cake with the cream cheese frosting.

Pina Colada Cake

Ingredients:

- 2 1/2 cups all-purpose flour
- 1 1/2 tsp baking powder
- 1/2 tsp salt
- 1 cup unsalted butter, softened
- 2 cups granulated sugar
- 4 large eggs
- 1 cup crushed pineapple, drained
- 1/2 cup coconut milk
- 1 tsp vanilla extract
- 1 cup shredded coconut

For the Frosting

- 8 oz cream cheese, softened
- 1/2 cup unsalted butter, softened
- 4 cups powdered sugar
- 1/4 cup coconut milk
- 1/2 cup shredded coconut

Instructions:

1. Preheat your oven to 350°F (175°C). Grease and flour two 9-inch round cake pans.
2. In a bowl, whisk together the flour, baking powder, and salt.
3. In a separate bowl, cream the butter and sugar together until light and fluffy.
4. Add the eggs, one at a time, beating well after each addition. Stir in the pineapple, coconut milk, and vanilla extract.
5. Gradually add the dry ingredients and fold in the shredded coconut.
6. Divide the batter between the pans and bake for 25-30 minutes, or until a toothpick inserted into the center comes out clean.
7. Let the cakes cool in the pans for 10 minutes, then transfer to a wire rack to cool completely.
8. For the frosting, beat the cream cheese and butter together until smooth. Gradually add the powdered sugar and coconut milk. Beat until fluffy.
9. Frost the cooled cake and top with shredded coconut.

Funfetti Bundt Cake

Ingredients:

- 2 1/2 cups all-purpose flour
- 2 tsp baking powder
- 1/2 tsp salt
- 1 cup unsalted butter, softened
- 2 cups granulated sugar
- 4 large eggs
- 1 tsp vanilla extract
- 1 cup whole milk
- 1/2 cup rainbow sprinkles

For the Glaze

- 1 cup powdered sugar
- 2 tbsp milk
- 1/2 tsp vanilla extract

Instructions:

1. Preheat your oven to 350°F (175°C). Grease and flour a 10-inch Bundt pan.
2. In a bowl, whisk together the flour, baking powder, and salt.
3. In a separate bowl, cream the butter and sugar together until light and fluffy.
4. Add the eggs, one at a time, beating well after each addition. Stir in the vanilla extract.
5. Gradually add the dry ingredients, alternating with the milk, until just combined.
6. Fold in the sprinkles.
7. Pour the batter into the prepared Bundt pan and smooth the top.
8. Bake for 45-50 minutes, or until a toothpick inserted into the center comes out clean.
9. Let the cake cool in the pan for 10 minutes, then transfer to a wire rack to cool completely.
10. For the glaze, whisk together the powdered sugar, milk, and vanilla extract until smooth. Drizzle over the cooled cake.

Chocolate Coconut Cake

Ingredients:

- 2 cups all-purpose flour
- 1 1/2 cups granulated sugar
- 1/2 cup unsweetened cocoa powder
- 1 tsp baking powder
- 1/2 tsp baking soda
- 1/2 tsp salt
- 1 cup buttermilk
- 1/2 cup unsalted butter, melted
- 2 large eggs
- 1 tsp vanilla extract
- 1 1/2 cups shredded coconut

For the Frosting

- 1 cup unsweetened cocoa powder
- 1/2 cup unsalted butter
- 1 cup powdered sugar
- 1/4 cup milk
- 1 tsp vanilla extract

Instructions:

1. Preheat your oven to 350°F (175°C). Grease and flour two 9-inch round cake pans.
2. In a bowl, whisk together the flour, sugar, cocoa powder, baking powder, baking soda, and salt.
3. In a separate bowl, whisk together the buttermilk, butter, eggs, and vanilla extract.
4. Gradually add the wet ingredients to the dry ingredients, mixing until just combined.
5. Fold in the shredded coconut.
6. Divide the batter between the prepared pans and bake for 25-30 minutes, or until a toothpick inserted into the center comes out clean.
7. Let the cakes cool in the pans for 10 minutes, then transfer to a wire rack to cool completely.

8. For the frosting, melt the butter in a saucepan over medium heat. Stir in the cocoa powder, powdered sugar, milk, and vanilla extract. Cook until smooth and thickened.
9. Frost the cooled cakes with the chocolate frosting.

Apple Cinnamon Cake

Ingredients:

- 2 cups all-purpose flour
- 1 1/2 tsp baking powder
- 1/2 tsp baking soda
- 1 tsp ground cinnamon
- 1/2 tsp salt
- 1/2 cup unsalted butter, softened
- 1 1/2 cups granulated sugar
- 2 large eggs
- 1 tsp vanilla extract
- 1 cup sour cream
- 2 cups peeled and chopped apples

For the Cinnamon Sugar Topping

- 1/4 cup granulated sugar
- 1 tsp ground cinnamon

Instructions:

1. Preheat your oven to 350°F (175°C). Grease and flour a 9-inch round cake pan.
2. In a bowl, whisk together the flour, baking powder, baking soda, cinnamon, and salt.
3. In a separate bowl, cream the butter and sugar together until light and fluffy.
4. Add the eggs, one at a time, beating well after each addition. Stir in the vanilla extract.
5. Gradually add the dry ingredients, alternating with the sour cream, until just combined.
6. Fold in the chopped apples.
7. Pour the batter into the prepared pan and smooth the top.
8. In a small bowl, mix together the sugar and cinnamon for the topping, then sprinkle over the top of the cake.
9. Bake for 30-35 minutes, or until a toothpick inserted into the center comes out clean.
10. Let the cake cool in the pan for 10 minutes, then transfer to a wire rack to cool completely.

Raspberry Almond Cake

Ingredients:

- 2 cups all-purpose flour
- 1 1/2 tsp baking powder
- 1/4 tsp salt
- 1/2 cup unsalted butter, softened
- 1 cup granulated sugar
- 2 large eggs
- 1 tsp vanilla extract
- 1 tsp almond extract
- 1/2 cup whole milk
- 1/2 cup fresh raspberries

For the Frosting

- 1/2 cup unsalted butter, softened
- 2 cups powdered sugar
- 1 tsp almond extract
- 1 tbsp milk

Instructions:

1. Preheat your oven to 350°F (175°C). Grease and flour two 9-inch round cake pans.
2. In a bowl, whisk together the flour, baking powder, and salt.
3. In a separate bowl, cream the butter and sugar together until light and fluffy.
4. Add the eggs, one at a time, beating well after each addition. Stir in the vanilla extract and almond extract.
5. Gradually add the dry ingredients, alternating with the milk, until just combined.
6. Gently fold in the raspberries.
7. Divide the batter between the pans and bake for 25-30 minutes, or until a toothpick inserted into the center comes out clean.
8. Let the cakes cool in the pans for 10 minutes, then transfer to a wire rack to cool completely.
9. For the frosting, beat the butter, powdered sugar, almond extract, and milk until smooth and fluffy.
10. Frost the cooled cakes with the almond frosting.

Black Forest Cake

Ingredients:

- 2 cups all-purpose flour
- 1 1/2 tsp baking powder
- 1/2 tsp baking soda
- 1/2 tsp salt
- 1 cup unsweetened cocoa powder
- 1 1/2 cups granulated sugar
- 2 large eggs
- 1 cup buttermilk
- 1/2 cup vegetable oil
- 1 tsp vanilla extract
- 1 cup cherries, pitted and chopped
- 1/2 cup maraschino cherries, drained

For the Frosting

- 2 cups heavy cream
- 2 tbsp powdered sugar
- 1 tsp vanilla extract

Instructions:

1. Preheat your oven to 350°F (175°C). Grease and flour two 9-inch round cake pans.
2. In a bowl, whisk together the flour, baking powder, baking soda, salt, and cocoa powder.
3. In a separate bowl, whisk together the sugar, eggs, buttermilk, oil, and vanilla extract.
4. Gradually add the dry ingredients to the wet ingredients, mixing until just combined.
5. Fold in the chopped cherries.
6. Divide the batter between the pans and bake for 25-30 minutes, or until a toothpick inserted into the center comes out clean.
7. Let the cakes cool in the pans for 10 minutes, then transfer to a wire rack to cool completely.
8. For the frosting, whip the heavy cream with the powdered sugar and vanilla extract until stiff peaks form.

9. Frost the cooled cakes with whipped cream, topping with maraschino cherries.

Hazelnut Cake with Chocolate Ganache

Ingredients:

- 2 cups all-purpose flour
- 1 1/2 tsp baking powder
- 1/2 tsp salt
- 1/2 cup unsalted butter, softened
- 1 cup granulated sugar
- 4 large eggs
- 1 tsp vanilla extract
- 1 cup ground hazelnuts
- 1/2 cup milk

For the Ganache

- 1 cup heavy cream
- 8 oz semisweet chocolate, chopped

Instructions:

1. Preheat your oven to 350°F (175°C). Grease and flour two 9-inch round cake pans.
2. In a bowl, whisk together the flour, baking powder, and salt.
3. In a separate bowl, cream the butter and sugar together until light and fluffy.
4. Add the eggs, one at a time, beating well after each addition. Stir in the vanilla extract.
5. Gradually add the dry ingredients, alternating with the milk, until just combined.
6. Fold in the ground hazelnuts.
7. Divide the batter between the pans and bake for 25-30 minutes, or until a toothpick inserted into the center comes out clean.
8. Let the cakes cool in the pans for 10 minutes, then transfer to a wire rack to cool completely.
9. For the ganache, heat the cream in a saucepan over medium heat until it just begins to boil. Pour over the chopped chocolate and let sit for 5 minutes. Stir until smooth.
10. Drizzle the ganache over the cooled cakes.

Snickerdoodle Cake

Ingredients:

- 2 cups all-purpose flour
- 1 1/2 tsp baking powder
- 1/2 tsp salt
- 1 tsp ground cinnamon
- 1/2 cup unsalted butter, softened
- 1 cup granulated sugar
- 2 large eggs
- 1 tsp vanilla extract
- 1 cup sour cream

For the Cinnamon Sugar Topping

- 1/4 cup granulated sugar
- 2 tsp ground cinnamon

Instructions:

1. Preheat your oven to 350°F (175°C). Grease and flour a 9-inch round cake pan.
2. In a bowl, whisk together the flour, baking powder, salt, and cinnamon.
3. In a separate bowl, cream the butter and sugar together until light and fluffy.
4. Add the eggs, one at a time, beating well after each addition. Stir in the vanilla extract.
5. Gradually add the dry ingredients, alternating with the sour cream, until just combined.
6. Pour the batter into the prepared pan.
7. In a small bowl, mix the cinnamon and sugar, then sprinkle it over the top of the cake.
8. Bake for 30-35 minutes, or until a toothpick inserted into the center comes out clean.
9. Let the cake cool in the pan for 10 minutes, then transfer to a wire rack to cool completely.

Lemon Blueberry Cake

Ingredients:

- 2 cups all-purpose flour
- 1 1/2 tsp baking powder
- 1/2 tsp salt
- 1/2 cup unsalted butter, softened
- 1 cup granulated sugar
- 3 large eggs
- 1 tsp vanilla extract
- 1 tbsp lemon zest
- 1/2 cup fresh lemon juice
- 1/2 cup buttermilk
- 1 cup fresh blueberries

For the Frosting

- 1 cup heavy cream
- 1/2 cup powdered sugar
- 1 tsp vanilla extract

Instructions:

1. Preheat your oven to 350°F (175°C). Grease and flour two 9-inch round cake pans.
2. In a bowl, whisk together the flour, baking powder, and salt.
3. In a separate bowl, cream the butter and sugar together until light and fluffy.
4. Add the eggs, one at a time, beating well after each addition. Stir in the vanilla extract, lemon zest, and lemon juice.
5. Gradually add the dry ingredients, alternating with the buttermilk, until just combined.
6. Gently fold in the blueberries.
7. Divide the batter between the pans and bake for 25-30 minutes, or until a toothpick inserted into the center comes out clean.
8. Let the cakes cool in the pans for 10 minutes, then transfer to a wire rack to cool completely.
9. For the frosting, whip the heavy cream with the powdered sugar and vanilla extract until stiff peaks form.
10. Frost the cooled cakes with whipped cream.

Vanilla Cupcakes with Buttercream Frosting

Ingredients:

- 1 1/2 cups all-purpose flour
- 1 1/2 tsp baking powder
- 1/4 tsp salt
- 1/2 cup unsalted butter, softened
- 1 cup granulated sugar
- 2 large eggs
- 1 tsp vanilla extract
- 1/2 cup whole milk

For the Buttercream Frosting

- 1/2 cup unsalted butter, softened
- 2 cups powdered sugar
- 1 tsp vanilla extract
- 2 tbsp milk

Instructions:

1. Preheat your oven to 350°F (175°C). Line a 12-cup muffin tin with paper liners.
2. In a bowl, whisk together the flour, baking powder, and salt.
3. In a separate bowl, cream the butter and sugar together until light and fluffy.
4. Add the eggs, one at a time, beating well after each addition. Stir in the vanilla extract.
5. Gradually add the dry ingredients, alternating with the milk, until just combined.
6. Divide the batter evenly among the muffin cups.
7. Bake for 18-20 minutes, or until a toothpick inserted into the center comes out clean.
8. Let the cupcakes cool completely.
9. For the frosting, beat the butter until smooth. Gradually add the powdered sugar, vanilla extract, and milk, beating until fluffy.
10. Frost the cooled cupcakes with buttercream.

Pistachio Cake

Ingredients:

- 2 cups all-purpose flour
- 1 1/2 tsp baking powder
- 1/4 tsp salt
- 1 cup unsalted butter, softened
- 1 cup granulated sugar
- 3 large eggs
- 1 tsp vanilla extract
- 1/2 cup buttermilk
- 1/2 cup finely ground pistachios

For the Frosting

- 1 cup heavy cream
- 1/2 cup powdered sugar
- 1/2 cup finely ground pistachios

Instructions:

1. Preheat your oven to 350°F (175°C). Grease and flour two 9-inch round cake pans.
2. In a bowl, whisk together the flour, baking powder, and salt.
3. In a separate bowl, cream the butter and sugar until light and fluffy.
4. Add the eggs, one at a time, mixing well after each addition. Stir in the vanilla extract.
5. Gradually add the dry ingredients, alternating with the buttermilk, until just combined.
6. Gently fold in the ground pistachios.
7. Divide the batter between the pans and bake for 25-30 minutes, or until a toothpick inserted into the center comes out clean.
8. Let the cakes cool in the pans for 10 minutes, then transfer to a wire rack to cool completely.
9. For the frosting, beat the heavy cream with the powdered sugar until stiff peaks form. Fold in the ground pistachios.
10. Frost the cooled cakes with the pistachio whipped cream.

Coconut Lime Cake

Ingredients:

- 2 cups all-purpose flour
- 1 1/2 tsp baking powder
- 1/2 tsp salt
- 1 cup unsalted butter, softened
- 1 cup granulated sugar
- 3 large eggs
- 1 tsp vanilla extract
- 1 tbsp lime zest
- 1/2 cup coconut milk
- 1/2 cup shredded coconut

For the Frosting

- 1 cup heavy cream
- 1/4 cup powdered sugar
- 2 tbsp lime juice
- 1/4 cup shredded coconut

Instructions:

1. Preheat your oven to 350°F (175°C). Grease and flour two 9-inch round cake pans.
2. In a bowl, whisk together the flour, baking powder, and salt.
3. In a separate bowl, cream the butter and sugar together until light and fluffy.
4. Add the eggs, one at a time, beating well after each addition. Stir in the vanilla extract and lime zest.
5. Gradually add the dry ingredients, alternating with the coconut milk, until just combined.
6. Fold in the shredded coconut.
7. Divide the batter between the pans and bake for 25-30 minutes, or until a toothpick comes out clean.
8. Let the cakes cool in the pans for 10 minutes, then transfer to a wire rack.
9. For the frosting, whip the heavy cream with powdered sugar and lime juice until stiff peaks form.
10. Frost the cooled cakes and top with shredded coconut.

Maple Pecan Cake

Ingredients:

- 2 cups all-purpose flour
- 1 1/2 tsp baking powder
- 1/4 tsp salt
- 1 cup unsalted butter, softened
- 1 cup packed brown sugar
- 3 large eggs
- 1 tsp vanilla extract
- 1/2 cup pure maple syrup
- 1/2 cup buttermilk
- 1 cup chopped pecans

For the Frosting

- 1 cup unsalted butter, softened
- 2 cups powdered sugar
- 1/4 cup maple syrup
- 1 tsp vanilla extract

Instructions:

1. Preheat your oven to 350°F (175°C). Grease and flour two 9-inch round cake pans.
2. In a bowl, whisk together the flour, baking powder, and salt.
3. In a separate bowl, cream the butter and brown sugar together until fluffy.
4. Add the eggs, one at a time, beating well after each addition. Stir in the vanilla extract and maple syrup.
5. Gradually add the dry ingredients, alternating with the buttermilk, until combined.
6. Fold in the chopped pecans.
7. Divide the batter between the pans and bake for 30-35 minutes, or until a toothpick comes out clean.
8. Let the cakes cool in the pans for 10 minutes, then transfer to a wire rack.
9. For the frosting, beat the butter until smooth. Gradually add powdered sugar, maple syrup, and vanilla, mixing until fluffy.
10. Frost the cooled cakes and garnish with chopped pecans.

Peach Cobbler Cake

Ingredients:

- 2 cups all-purpose flour
- 1 1/2 tsp baking powder
- 1/4 tsp salt
- 1 cup unsalted butter, softened
- 1 cup granulated sugar
- 3 large eggs
- 1 tsp vanilla extract
- 1 cup fresh or canned peach slices, drained and chopped

For the Topping

- 1/4 cup granulated sugar
- 1/2 tsp cinnamon

Instructions:

1. Preheat your oven to 350°F (175°C). Grease and flour a 9-inch round cake pan.
2. In a bowl, whisk together the flour, baking powder, and salt.
3. In another bowl, cream the butter and sugar until light and fluffy.
4. Add the eggs, one at a time, beating well after each addition. Stir in the vanilla extract.
5. Gradually add the dry ingredients until just combined.
6. Gently fold in the chopped peaches.
7. Pour the batter into the prepared pan.
8. Mix the sugar and cinnamon for the topping and sprinkle it over the batter.
9. Bake for 35-40 minutes, or until a toothpick inserted comes out clean.
10. Let the cake cool before serving.

Nutella Swirl Cake

Ingredients:

- 2 cups all-purpose flour
- 1 1/2 tsp baking powder
- 1/4 tsp salt
- 1 cup unsalted butter, softened
- 1 cup granulated sugar
- 3 large eggs
- 1 tsp vanilla extract
- 1/2 cup whole milk
- 1/2 cup Nutella

For the Ganache

- 1/2 cup heavy cream
- 1/2 cup Nutella

Instructions:

1. Preheat your oven to 350°F (175°C). Grease and flour a 9-inch round cake pan.
2. In a bowl, whisk together the flour, baking powder, and salt.
3. In a separate bowl, cream the butter and sugar together until light and fluffy.
4. Add the eggs, one at a time, mixing well after each addition. Stir in the vanilla extract.
5. Gradually add the dry ingredients, alternating with the milk, until just combined.
6. Swirl in the Nutella by adding spoonfuls of Nutella to the batter and gently swirling with a knife.
7. Bake for 30-35 minutes, or until a toothpick comes out clean.
8. For the ganache, heat the cream in a saucepan until it simmers, then stir in Nutella until smooth.
9. Drizzle the ganache over the cooled cake.

Churro Cake

Ingredients:

- 2 cups all-purpose flour
- 1 1/2 tsp baking powder
- 1/4 tsp salt
- 1 tsp cinnamon
- 1 cup unsalted butter, softened
- 1 cup granulated sugar
- 3 large eggs
- 1 tsp vanilla extract
- 1/2 cup buttermilk

For the Topping

- 1/4 cup granulated sugar
- 2 tsp cinnamon

Instructions:

1. Preheat your oven to 350°F (175°C). Grease and flour a 9-inch round cake pan.
2. In a bowl, whisk together the flour, baking powder, salt, and cinnamon.
3. In another bowl, cream the butter and sugar together until light and fluffy.
4. Add the eggs, one at a time, mixing well after each addition. Stir in the vanilla extract.
5. Gradually add the dry ingredients, alternating with the buttermilk, until just combined.
6. Pour the batter into the prepared pan and bake for 30-35 minutes.
7. Mix the sugar and cinnamon for the topping and sprinkle over the cake while it's still warm.
8. Let the cake cool completely.

White Chocolate Raspberry Cake

Ingredients:

- 2 cups all-purpose flour
- 1 1/2 tsp baking powder
- 1/4 tsp salt
- 1 cup unsalted butter, softened
- 1 cup granulated sugar
- 3 large eggs
- 1 tsp vanilla extract
- 1/2 cup buttermilk
- 1/2 cup white chocolate chips
- 1 cup fresh raspberries

For the Frosting

- 1 cup heavy cream
- 1/2 cup white chocolate chips

Instructions:

1. Preheat your oven to 350°F (175°C). Grease and flour two 9-inch round cake pans.
2. In a bowl, whisk together the flour, baking powder, and salt.
3. In a separate bowl, cream the butter and sugar until fluffy.
4. Add the eggs, one at a time, beating well after each addition. Stir in vanilla extract.
5. Gradually add the dry ingredients, alternating with the buttermilk.
6. Fold in the white chocolate chips and raspberries.
7. Divide the batter and bake for 25-30 minutes.
8. For the frosting, heat the heavy cream and white chocolate chips until melted. Whisk until smooth.
9. Frost the cooled cakes with the white chocolate ganache.

Double Chocolate Chip Cake

Ingredients:

- 1 3/4 cups all-purpose flour
- 1 1/2 tsp baking powder
- 1/4 tsp salt
- 1/2 cup unsweetened cocoa powder
- 1 cup unsalted butter, softened
- 1 cup granulated sugar
- 3 large eggs
- 1 tsp vanilla extract
- 1/2 cup whole milk
- 1 cup chocolate chips

For the Ganache

- 1/2 cup heavy cream
- 1/2 cup semisweet chocolate chips

Instructions:

1. Preheat your oven to 350°F (175°C). Grease and flour two 9-inch round cake pans.
2. In a bowl, whisk together the flour, baking powder, salt, and cocoa powder.
3. In a separate bowl, cream the butter and sugar together until light and fluffy.
4. Add the eggs, one at a time, mixing well after each addition. Stir in the vanilla extract.
5. Gradually add the dry ingredients, alternating with the milk, until just combined.
6. Fold in the chocolate chips.
7. Bake for 25-30 minutes, or until a toothpick comes out clean.
8. For the ganache, heat the cream until it simmers, then pour over the chocolate chips. Stir until smooth.
9. Drizzle the ganache over the cooled cakes.

Pumpkin Spice Cake

Ingredients:

- 2 cups all-purpose flour
- 1 1/2 tsp baking powder
- 1/2 tsp baking soda
- 1 1/2 tsp cinnamon
- 1/2 tsp ground nutmeg
- 1/4 tsp ground ginger
- 1/4 tsp salt
- 1 cup unsalted butter, softened
- 1 cup granulated sugar
- 3 large eggs
- 1 cup canned pumpkin puree
- 1 tsp vanilla extract

For the Cream Cheese Frosting

- 8 oz cream cheese, softened
- 1/4 cup unsalted butter, softened
- 2 cups powdered sugar
- 1 tsp vanilla extract

Instructions:

1. Preheat your oven to 350°F (175°C). Grease and flour a 9-inch round cake pan.
2. In a bowl, whisk together the flour, baking powder, baking soda, cinnamon, nutmeg, ginger, and salt.
3. In a separate bowl, cream the butter and sugar until fluffy.
4. Add the eggs, one at a time, beating well after each addition. Stir in the pumpkin puree and vanilla extract.
5. Gradually add the dry ingredients, mixing until just combined.
6. Pour the batter into the prepared pan and bake for 30-35 minutes.
7. For the frosting, beat the cream cheese and butter until smooth. Gradually add powdered sugar and vanilla extract, mixing until fluffy.
8. Frost the cooled cake.

Mocha Hazelnut Cake

Ingredients:

- 2 cups all-purpose flour
- 1 1/2 tsp baking powder
- 1/4 tsp salt
- 1/2 cup unsweetened cocoa powder
- 1 cup unsalted butter, softened
- 1 cup granulated sugar
- 3 large eggs
- 1 tsp vanilla extract
- 1/2 cup brewed coffee
- 1/2 cup hazelnut spread

For the Ganache

- 1/2 cup heavy cream
- 1/2 cup semisweet chocolate chips

Instructions:

1. Preheat your oven to 350°F (175°C). Grease and flour two 9-inch round cake pans.
2. In a bowl, whisk together the flour, baking powder, salt, and cocoa powder.
3. In a separate bowl, cream the butter and sugar together until light and fluffy.
4. Add the eggs, one at a time, mixing well after each addition. Stir in the vanilla extract and brewed coffee.
5. Gradually add the dry ingredients until just combined.
6. Fold in the hazelnut spread.
7. Divide the batter and bake for 25-30 minutes.
8. For the ganache, heat the heavy cream and chocolate chips until melted.
9. Frost the cooled cakes with ganache.

Cream Puff Cake

Ingredients:

For the Cake:

- 1 cup water
- 1/2 cup unsalted butter
- 1 cup all-purpose flour
- 1/4 tsp salt
- 4 large eggs

For the Filling:

- 2 cups heavy whipping cream
- 8 oz cream cheese (softened)
- 1/4 cup powdered sugar
- 1 tsp vanilla extract

For the Topping:

- Powdered sugar (for dusting)

Instructions:

1. Prepare the Cake:

- Preheat your oven to 400°F (200°C). Grease a 9x13-inch baking dish or line it with parchment paper.
- In a medium saucepan, combine the water and butter over medium heat. Stir until the butter is melted and the mixture comes to a boil.
- Once boiling, remove from the heat and stir in the flour and salt. Mix well until it forms a smooth dough.
- Add the eggs one at a time, beating well after each addition. The dough should be thick and smooth.
- Spread the dough evenly into the prepared baking dish.
- Bake for 25-30 minutes or until the cake is puffed and golden brown. Allow it to cool completely.

2. Prepare the Filling:

- In a large mixing bowl, beat the heavy whipping cream until stiff peaks form. Set aside.
- In another bowl, beat the softened cream cheese with the powdered sugar and vanilla extract until smooth and creamy.
- Gently fold the whipped cream into the cream cheese mixture until well combined.

3. Assemble the Cake:

- Once the cake has cooled, spread the cream filling evenly over the top.
- Use a dusting of powdered sugar over the filling to finish.

4. Serve:

- Slice the cream puff cake into squares and serve chilled. The texture should be light and fluffy with a smooth, creamy filling.

Chocolate Mint Cake

Ingredients:

- **For the cake:**
    - 1 3/4 cups all-purpose flour
    - 1 1/2 cups granulated sugar
    - 1/2 cup unsweetened cocoa powder
    - 1 tsp baking powder
    - 1 1/2 tsp baking soda
    - 1 tsp salt
    - 2 large eggs
    - 1 cup whole milk
    - 1/2 cup vegetable oil
    - 2 tsp vanilla extract
    - 1 cup boiling water
    - 1/2 cup chopped mint chocolate or mint chips
- **For the mint frosting:**
    - 1/2 cup unsalted butter, softened
    - 4 cups powdered sugar
    - 2-3 tbsp heavy cream
    - 1 tsp peppermint extract
    - Green food coloring (optional)

Instructions:

1. Preheat your oven to 350°F (175°C). Grease and flour two 9-inch round cake pans.
2. In a large bowl, combine flour, sugar, cocoa powder, baking powder, baking soda, and salt.
3. Add eggs, milk, oil, and vanilla extract to the dry ingredients. Mix until smooth.
4. Slowly add the boiling water to the batter, mixing until well combined. The batter will be thin.
5. Pour the batter into the prepared pans and bake for 30-35 minutes or until a toothpick inserted into the center comes out clean. Let cool completely.
6. For the frosting, beat together butter, powdered sugar, cream, peppermint extract, and food coloring until smooth and fluffy.
7. Frost the cooled cakes with the mint frosting and sprinkle with chopped mint chocolate or mint chips.

Cinnamon Roll Cake

Ingredients:

- **For the cake:**
    - 1 1/2 cups all-purpose flour
    - 1 cup granulated sugar
    - 1/2 tsp baking powder
    - 1/2 tsp baking soda
    - 1/2 tsp salt
    - 1 cup buttermilk
    - 1/2 cup unsalted butter, melted
    - 1 tsp vanilla extract
    - 2 large eggs
- **For the cinnamon swirl:**
    - 1/2 cup brown sugar
    - 1 tbsp ground cinnamon
    - 2 tbsp unsalted butter, melted
- **For the glaze:**
    - 1 cup powdered sugar
    - 2 tbsp milk
    - 1 tsp vanilla extract

Instructions:

1. Preheat the oven to 350°F (175°C) and grease a 9x13-inch baking pan.
2. In a bowl, mix flour, sugar, baking powder, baking soda, and salt.
3. In another bowl, whisk together buttermilk, melted butter, vanilla extract, and eggs. Combine with the dry ingredients until smooth.
4. For the cinnamon swirl, mix brown sugar and cinnamon. Pour half the batter into the pan, then sprinkle with the cinnamon-sugar mixture and top with the remaining batter.
5. Swirl the batter with a knife to create a marble effect.
6. Bake for 35-40 minutes, until a toothpick comes out clean.
7. For the glaze, mix powdered sugar, milk, and vanilla extract. Drizzle over the cake while still warm.

Chocolate Cherry Cake

Ingredients:

- **For the cake:**
    - 1 box chocolate cake mix
    - 1 cup sour cream
    - 1/2 cup vegetable oil
    - 3 large eggs
    - 1 tsp vanilla extract
    - 1 cup chopped cherries (fresh or maraschino)
- **For the frosting:**
    - 1/2 cup unsalted butter, softened
    - 3 cups powdered sugar
    - 2-3 tbsp milk
    - 1/4 cup cocoa powder
    - 1/2 cup chopped cherries

Instructions:

1. Preheat the oven to 350°F (175°C) and grease a 9x13-inch baking pan.
2. In a large bowl, mix the chocolate cake mix, sour cream, vegetable oil, eggs, and vanilla extract until smooth. Fold in the chopped cherries.
3. Pour the batter into the pan and bake for 30-35 minutes or until a toothpick comes out clean.
4. For the frosting, beat the butter with powdered sugar, cocoa powder, and milk until smooth. Fold in the chopped cherries.
5. Frost the cooled cake with the cherry chocolate frosting.

Chocolate Raspberry Bundt Cake

Ingredients:

- **For the cake:**
    - 1 1/2 cups all-purpose flour
    - 1 1/2 tsp baking powder
    - 1/2 tsp baking soda
    - 1/4 tsp salt
    - 1/2 cup unsweetened cocoa powder
    - 1 cup granulated sugar
    - 1/2 cup unsalted butter, softened
    - 2 large eggs
    - 1 tsp vanilla extract
    - 1/2 cup sour cream
    - 1/2 cup fresh raspberries, mashed
    - 1/2 cup milk
- **For the ganache:**
    - 1 cup heavy cream
    - 8 oz semisweet chocolate, chopped
    - 1/2 tsp vanilla extract

Instructions:

1. Preheat the oven to 350°F (175°C) and grease a bundt pan.
2. In a medium bowl, mix the flour, baking powder, baking soda, salt, and cocoa powder.
3. In a separate bowl, cream the butter and sugar until light and fluffy. Add the eggs one at a time, beating well after each.
4. Add the vanilla extract and mix well. Gradually add the flour mixture alternately with sour cream, raspberries, and milk until smooth.
5. Pour the batter into the bundt pan and bake for 45-50 minutes or until a toothpick comes out clean.
6. For the ganache, heat the cream in a saucepan until it begins to simmer. Pour it over the chopped chocolate and stir until smooth. Add the vanilla extract.
7. Drizzle the ganache over the cooled bundt cake.

www.ingramcontent.com/pod-product-compliance
Lightning Source LLC
LaVergne TN
LVHW081322060526
838201LV00055B/2402